Thing Will Sing

and

King Biff and the Gong

PHASE 3

/th/ng/

Level 3 – Yellow

Helpful Hints for Reading at Home

The graphemes (written letters) and phonemes (units of sound) used throughout this series are aligned with Letters and Sounds. This offers a consistent approach to learning whether reading at home or in the classroom.

HERE IS A LIST OF PHONEMES FOR THIS PHASE OF LEARNING. AN EXAMPLE OF THE PRONUNCIATION CAN BE FOUND IN BRACKETS.

Phase 3			
j (jug)	v (van)	w (wet)	x (fox)
y (yellow)	z (zoo)	zz (buzz)	qu (quick)
ch (chip)	sh (shop)	th (thin/then)	ng (ring)
ai (rain)	ee (feet)	igh (night)	oa (boat)
oo (boot/look)	ar (farm)	or (for)	ur (hurt)
ow (cow)	oi (coin)	ear (dear)	air (fair)
ure (sure)	er (corner)		

HERE ARE SOME WORDS WHICH YOUR CHILD MAY FIND TRICKY.

Phase 3 Tricky Words			
he	you	she	they
we	all	me	are
be	my	was	her

TOP TIPS FOR HELPING YOUR CHILD TO READ:

• Allow children time to break down unfamiliar words into units of sound and then encourage children to string these sounds together to create the word.

• Encourage your child to point out any focus phonics when they are used.

• Read through the book more than once to grow confidence.

• Ask simple questions about the text to assess understanding.

• Encourage children to use illustrations as prompts.

This book focuses on the phonemes /th/ and /ng/ and is a yellow level 3 book band.

Thing Will Sing

and

King Biff and the Gong

Written by
Mignonne Gunasekara

Illustrated by
Danielle Webster-Jones

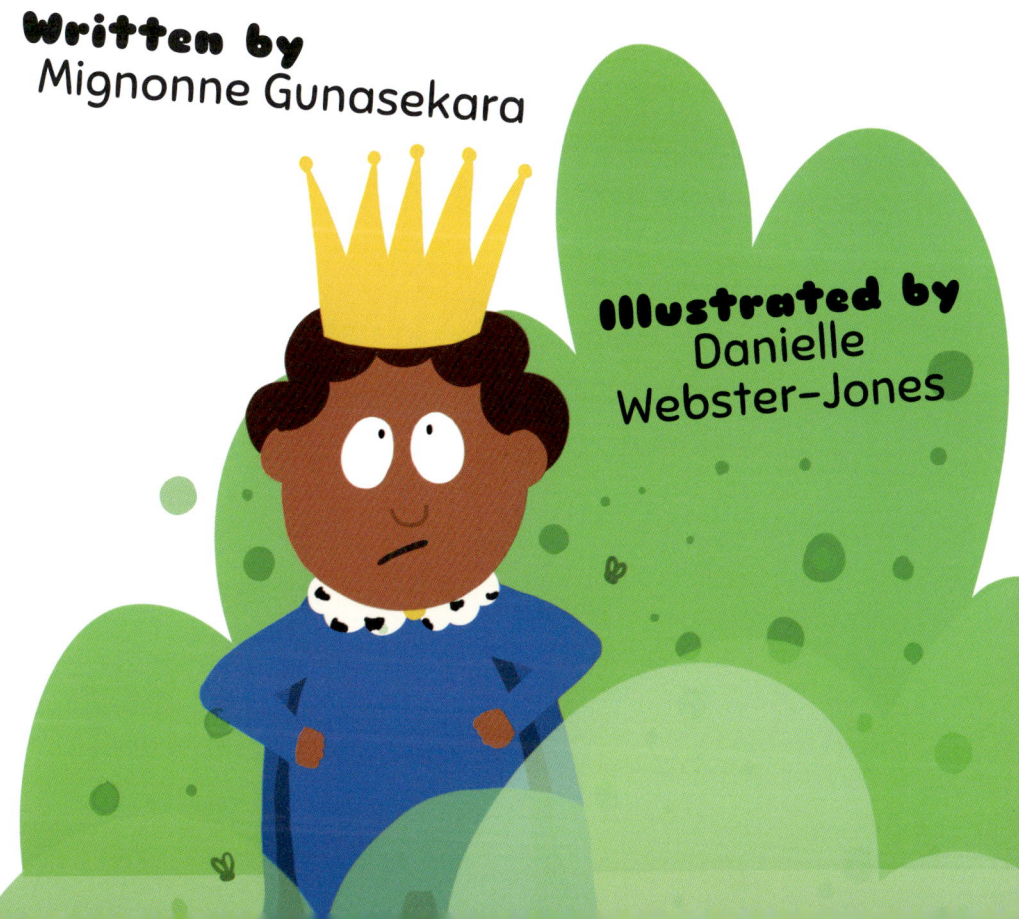

Can you say this sound and draw it with your finger?

Thing Will Sing

Written by
Mignonne Gunasekara

Illustrated by
Danielle Webster-Jones

This is Thing. He has a song to sing.

Thing rings his pals, but they will not pick up.

"I will go to them," Thing yells.

Thing is off to get his pals.

Are they in the bin? Are they on the van?

"My pals! Can I sing my song?"

"No, Thing. You can not sing."

"But it is a rad song! Let me sing."

Thing is mad. This will not do!

Thing has to sing his song!

No. This is not a song…

This is a yell! Aaaaaaaaaaaaaaaah!

Can you say this sound and draw it with your finger?

King Biff and the Gong

Written by
Mignonne Gunasekara

Illustrated by
Danielle Webster-Jones

Biff is a king. King Biff pongs.

King Biff has a gong. This is the gong. Bong!

The gong tells King Biff to get in the tub.

But King Biff is not a fan of the tub.

Quick! Bang on the gong! Bing! Bang! Bong!

"Get rid of that pong in the tub, King Biff!"

"I am the king! I will pong for as long as I can!"

King Biff is mad. The gong bongs.
King Biff runs.

But he can not run for long.
They are on him.

"I will get rid of that bad, bad gong!"

"The gong has to go!" King Biff yells.

The king rams the gong. So long, gong!

©2022 **BookLife Publishing Ltd.**
King's Lynn, Norfolk, PE30 4LS, UK

ISBN 978-1-80155-470-1
All rights reserved. Printed in Poland.
A catalogue record for this book is available from the British Library.

Thing Will Sing and King Biff and the Gong
Written by Mignonne Gunasekara
Illustrated by Danielle Webster-Jones

An Introduction to BookLife Readers...

Our Readers have been specifically created in line with the London Institute of Education's approach to book banding and are phonetically decodable and ordered to support each phase of Letters and Sounds.

Each book has been created to provide the best possible reading and learning experience. Our aim is to share our love of books with children, providing both emerging readers and prolific page-turners with beautiful books that are guaranteed to provoke interest and learning, regardless of ability.

BOOK BAND GRADED using the Institute of Education's approach to levelling.

PHONETICALLY DECODABLE supporting each phase of Letters and Sounds.

EXERCISES AND QUESTIONS to offer reinforcement and to ascertain comprehension.

BEAUTIFULLY ILLUSTRATED to inspire and provoke engagement, providing a variety of styles for the reader to enjoy whilst reading through the series.

AUTHOR INSIGHT:
MIGNONNE GUNASEKARA

Born in Sri Lanka, Mignonne has always been drawn to stories, whether they are told through literature, film or music. After studying Biomedical Science at King's College London, Mignonne completed a short course in screenwriting at the National Centre for Writing in Norwich, during which she explored writing scripts for the different mediums of film, theatre and radio.

This book focuses on the phonemes /th/ and /ng/ and is a yellow level 3 book band.